© Uzochukwu Mike P 2020

Published by:

Smart Connect

All rights reserved. No part of this publication may be reproduced, stored in a retrieval system, or transmitted in any form or by any means, electronic, mechanical, photocopying, recording, or otherwise, without the prior written permission of the author.

DEDICATION

This book is dedicated to my only sister in the person of Okwuagbala Chinwe Dorothy.

ACKNOWLEDGEMENTS

My first acknowledgement goes to the manager of my unit at FBN Insurance, Retail Sales Manager Ekhator Godwin Imariagbe. You are such a good manager and I would not have completed this book without your contribution as you fed me with the basic information I needed to get this job done. I acknowledge my family members, team members of FBN Insurance Abraka Unit, the staff of First Bank of Nigeria Abraka branch of Nigeria and my well wishers.

TABLE OF CONTENTS

Chapter 1

Introduction to Insurance Managers

Insurance being an important area of concentration has managers that supervise the activities of the salesmen, customers and the company in general. These managers work in a way that they will meet the target given to them by the company. In the course of making sure that things are put in place, they react differently. There are many kinds of insurance unit managers and they are differentiated by their characters.

As the head office mounts pressure on these managers, they push the pressure to the salesmen. They may keep threatening the salespersons that they will lose their jobs of they do not buckle up in their duties. This is one of the reasons why many persons said they cannot work in any insurance company. They do not want to absorb any form of pressure that may come from any head.

Location is another thing that can make a manager either successful or not. Though it depends on what being successful may imply to any individual because there are many managers who are successful irrespective of the fact that they find themselves in a society where economic activities are not high when compared with other locations. Many insurance managers said they are more successful than others because of the location they occupy.

There are managers who do less of their office works. They feel they do not need to be in the office always because they have worked for the company for a long time to attain such managerial position. Something outside the office takes their attentions. Some of them have businesses which they manage on their own. As a result of this, such businesses always take their attentions.

Some at that point of their managerial career pay more attention to their families. They become absent from work to attend to their families need. But these attitudes are observed in countries or communities where the activities of these men and women are not monitored. If there are strong monitoring teams that check on these managers, such will not happen.

1.1 Levels of Insurance Managers

In the managerial positions of insurance services, there are specific levels of managers. These individual managers make sure they do their basic functions to keep their appointment with the company that employed them. But no matter the level occupied by any manager in the insurance industry, they are the big bosses in the company. Also, it is important to understand that a manager can be in a particular level and still gain promotion which increases his earnings in return. The levels of insurance managers are as follow:

(1) Unit Manager or Retail Sales Manager

(2) Senior Sales Manager (SSM)

(3) Area Sales Manager (ASM)

Unit Manager

The unit manager in the retail section of an insurance office oversees the activities of the salespersons. He guides insurance agents that are under his care. He uses his managerial skills to direct the salesmen on how to make sales and get positive results in the job they do. They are respected by the salespersons that work under them.

A unit manager in a particular branch of an insurance company can have maximum of 20 salespersons working under his care. The twenty persons report to him every week to submit their customers' proposal forms to him. He signs the proposal forms and makes sure that everything is in place before the policies are captured and converted. It is after the capturing and conversation of the policies that commission is paid to the agents on those businesses.

Senior Sales Manager (SSM)

The Senior Sales Manager leads and manages all sales operations and oversees activities of the junior sales management team. The key objective of the Senior Sales Manager is to grow incremental and new sales for the business while simultaneously reducing customer turnover. The Senior Sales Manager builds and manages all aspects of a sales department inclusive of leading management, account management, business analytics, and channel development (Cleverism 2016).

In insurance, senior sales manager heads unit managers. In most cases, a senior sales manager was once a unit manager. It was when promoted in the managerial position that he became a senior sales manager. The unit managers take instructions from the SSM.

In a religion which involves many states, there can be more than 4 senior sales managers depending on the number of states that make up such region. Let us take for example that there are two states that make up a region, there can be two senior sales managers in the region. One oversees the insurance activities that go on in one state while the other takes care of the other state. But know that the way a region is grouped is depending on a particular insurance company.

Promotion from an ordinary sales manager to a senior sales manager is dependent on some factors. These factors include the experience one has had in the job, the productivity of the manager, the managerial duration he has had, and the performance of the salespersons under him.

Area Sales Manager (ASM)

An area sales manager is the big boss in the insurance industry. His voice is heard in a big way whenever he speaks. Some fearful unit managers tremble whenever the area sales manager speaks in any location he is. He earns big amount of money in the insurance company and lives big at the same time.

As an area sales manager, you'll be responsible for overseeing the sales operation of your company in a particular geographical area. This could well include several counties, so expect to be fairly busy (Total Jobs 2009). An area sales manager covers much in any insurance company he finds his or herself.

An area sales manager makes sure he drives the consumption of the products of the company. He works hard to improve the customer base of the company by creating avenues to bring in new customers into the company while maintaining the existence of the old ones. He sometimes oversees more than one state depending on the geographical division of the company.

An area sales manager develops sales strategies and set targets. He sets target for unit managers who use their positions to enforce such target on the insurance salespersons. Apart from the normal target given by the company, an area sales manager sets his own and makes it higher. He wants the workers to make more sales for the company so that he can earn more commission and win awards.

In terms of learning, an area sales manager is sometimes mandated to learn more in sales and marketing. The insurance company where they work sometimes sponsor them to learn more on the area of interest within the country and sometimes outside the country. The company do this because they want their officers to be grounded academically in the job position they occupy. The courses can include Chartered Institute of Marketing (CIM), Advanced Certificate in Sales Management Diploma in Professional Sales, Institute of Sales and Marketing Management (ISMM), and Level 5 Diploma in Strategic Sales (Sales Management or Key Account Management).

In summary on the area sales manager, an area sales manager typically manages sales force within his defined regional territory. He or she is responsible for overseeing sales operations, meeting targets and managing the sales team in the region. He heads both the unit managers and senior sales managers.

References

- Cleverism (2016), Senior Sales Manager, published by Cleverism
- Total Jobs (2009), Area sales manager job description, published by Total Jobs Group Ltd, Southwark Street, London, England

Chapter 2

Attaining Managerial Position in Insurance Company

The target of many insurance agents is to move from the level of being ordinary salespersons to the level of unit managers. Everyone wants to grow though some agents on the other hand still do not want such positions as managers. Some want to become executive salespersons or executive financial advisors. They have their reasons for that. Some salespersons will tell you that they do not want to become managers because they still want to have their freedom.

Also, some agents believe they do not have leadership skills and therefore cannot head any unit as manager. People have their believe and reasons for not applying for managerial positions when there are opportunities for them to apply. Many salespersons also believe they cannot absorb the pressure that may come from the company in regards to meeting of target when they assume managerial positions.

Working to demanding sales targets can be challenging, although the financial rewards can be good for those who enjoy this type of work. That is for those that assume the leadership position in any insurance company. They work hard with their agents to meet up the target expected of them. The thing is that once they are meeting the target expected from them in terms of production, they smile as they are paid.

Many insurance managers are happy being addressed as managers. Some are happy because of the fact that they receive more money in that position than when they were ordinary marketers in the company. And another reason is because they are happy being addressed as managers. Many people like being respected as titles are added before their names.

2.1 Criteria for becoming an Insurance Manager

Many may aspire to become managers in many insurance companies. These aspirations are not bad because everyone wants to find his or herself on the top. But there are criteria for attaining such position. The criteria to become a unit manager in any insurance company are as follow:

(1) The years spent in the company

(2) The productivity of the agent

(3) Total premium brought

(4) Persistency rate of customers in premium payment

(5) Number of lapsed cases

(6) Boldness and the ability to lead a Team

The Years spent in the Company

Some insurance companies do not hire any person who has spent few years in the company to head a particular group of people. Also, many insurance companies do not hire any salesperson that has not spent over two years from another insurance company. The reason for this is because people who spend less number of years in sales may not understand the products properly.

In so many job vacancies on insurance managerial position, years of experience is one of the areas capitalized on. The longer a person stays in a particular area of discipline, the more experience the person gains in the field. The manager is to handle many people and because of that need to have good experience on the job. So, if you are aspiring to be a manager in any insurance company, know that you have to spend certain number of years in the insurance industry. Even if you want to move from the insurance company where you work to another insurance company, you must have spent certain number of years in the insurance company.

According to Dan MCCarthy (2018), "Manager. Five to ten years of experience required. Proven track record of effective management" According to the author, effective managers suppose to have spent that number of years of experience before assuming managerial position. But some companies have something less than that as one of their major criteria.

The Productivity of the Agent

How many proposal forms have the agent that is applying for the position of unit manager submitted since he or she started to work in that particular insurance company? That is the question the interviewers usually ask when the person applying for the position of a unit manager is from the same company. The essence of the question is to know whether the agent is really productive and can lead the persons yet to be handed over to his or her care.

There is a statement that someone cannot give what he or she does not have. Also, insurance companies believe that a lion gives birth to a lion. That is the reason why insurance companies are interested on the number of proposal forms an aspirant into managerial position has given the company since inception.

In insurance company, production leads to promotion. If you produce consistently, there is higher possibility of getting the position of unit manager in the company. So, insurance agents that want to become managers in the long run as they continue with their business of marketing are advised by the company to make more sales.

The kind of products that the agent sells to the clients is still important. In Life Insurance Company for instance, agents usually sell more endowment and savings products. These are products that are sellable without much stress. But not withstanding that, life insurance companies encourage the sales of risk products. Risk products are pure life insurance products.

They are products that cover mainly the life of the assured. In the case of the death of the life assured, the claim is paid to the beneficiary. If there is no death of the policyholder for that duration of the coverage, none of the premiums paid by the life assured is returned.

That is another criterion that the Life Insurance Companies use. The products and the kinds of products sold by an agent that applies for managerial position matter. Why insurance companies pay attention to this is because that is what insurance company is mainly known for irrespective of other new products in the market today that encourage savings more than life cover.

Sometimes, some insurance companies design some products at a particular point in time. They want these new products sold to prospects outside there. Managerial aspirants who have sold these new products usually have edge over others that apply for the same job.

Total Premium brought into the company

This is one of the criteria that insurance companies use whenever they are choosing any of their agents for the position of a manager. They calculate to know how the agent applying for that precious position has contributed to the development of the company financially.

Insurance companies are business set up by group of people with common goal. The difference between it and someone that run an individual business set up is on number. Insurance usually involve group of people that join their capital and resources to achieve a particular result.

Before an individual gives some gifts to certain customers, those customers have to be exceptional. They may be the people that have been buying from the business owner for a long time. What it implies is that such customers have contributed much money to the growth of the man's business.

The same applies when it comes to promotion in insurance company. They check to know how much each individual has contributed to know if he or she deserves the position. They are all businessmen and women. Financial contribution into the company is important to them as well.

In choosing an agent to be manager of any unit in insurance company, the gift he or she receives from the insurance company is the managerial position in respect to an individual business owner that gives items as gifts. One of the reasons why insurance companies look at the total premiums an agent has brought into the company is to know if such person can drive his team to make more money for the company when chosen as a new manager. Insurance companies are in competition with others and one of the ways to grow stronger is when they have good financial base.

Companies offering products and services in the general insurance market are believed to trade under very competitive conditions (Gulumser Murat, Roger S. Tonkin and D. Johannes Jüttner 2002). Insurance companies operating in an increasingly competitive market must innovate and be proactive to prosper (Gonzalo Vina 2017). According to Gonzalo, insurance companies do not only have to be innovative but also be proactive. And one of the measures applied when screening workers to be appointed into managerial position is to know how proactive they have been by checking how much they have brought into the company.

Any of the agents who have not contributed satisfactorily in terms of premium is not likely to be eligible for such position. There is a particular total premium required but it is dependent on the insurance company. It also varies per year of fresh recruitment of salespersons into managerial position.

In the appointment of salespersons into managerial position conducted by a region of FBN Insurance in 2019, the measure used by the company was that any aspirant must have total premium of thirty million Nigerian naira (N30,000,000) paid by his or her total clients. Any aspirant whose customers' total premium paid is less than that was not eligible to contest. The money aspect is important.

Persistency Rate of Customers in Premium Payment

One thing is to bring customers into an insurance company and another thing is to maintain these customers. That is where the work lies and many insurance agents have failed in this area. Many agents are after closing of many insurance deals but lack the ability to maintain them. Some cannot even recognize the person they sold insurance policy to when they meet them three months after or more. Insurance managements do not just want you to sell their products alone. They want you to sell and at the same time make sure those customers are paying their premiums as of when due. Insurance industry frowns at lapsed cases. They know that if large numbers of your customers are paying, the coverage on the insured will be active and they will make more money at the same time.

In selecting a salesperson into the position of manager, one of the areas considered is the persistency rate of the agent's line of customers in premium payment. If this is not scored up to average, the applicant is likely to lose the job. There are reasons why insurance companies look at this criterion before appointing an ordinary insurance salesperson into the position of retails sales manager.

One thing is that the top officials want to know whether the agent has been mis-selling the company's product. The company believes that one of the reasons that can make an agent's line of customers to stop paying their premiums is because they were not sold to rightly. Maybe along the line when the customers found out the truth behind that particular policy, they stopped paying. So, no insurance company will like to handover some persons of about 20 or more into the hands of someone that has not been representing the company well.

The board of directors of the company know they will be in big trouble if they do so. They would not like to take such foolish risk because it can dent the image of the company. If such agent is appointed to lead a group of people, the people he will lead have higher chances of mis-selling as well. The reason is because their new manager was guilty of mis-selling and can influence the agents under him to do same.

Many agents have sold to wrong people over the years. Some have murdered the endowment plans designed by their insurance companies. They did this because they sold some endowment policies to people they know could not continue with the policy in the long run. They want to have many proposal forms submitted every week and ended up selling to the wrong persons. Some sold 6 years endowment plan to students whom they know would hardly eat three square meals a day not to talk of paying monthly premiums.

This makes many agents to have more that 60% of their customers' line not paying their premiums persistently. That is to say that such salesperson has customers' persistency rate of just 40%. An agent with this kind of record can hardly get a managerial position in the company he or she works.

Some agents have maintained clean sheet but failed in this area. If you are an agent planning to head a unit as a manager tomorrow, you have to make sure that your customers premium payment persistency rate is high. It will help you have edge over many other aspirants and applicants for the same position.

Number of lapsed Cases

This subtitle can also be called number of lapsed policies. When is a policy said to have been lapsed? The policy for which all benefits to the policy holder cease and is terminated due to non payment of premium amount on the due date or even after the grace period is called a lapsed policy (The Economic Times 2016).

In many life insurance companies, a policy lapses after one year of none payment of premium amount agreed at the commencement of the policy. Insurance companies are unhappy seeing large number of their customers not making payments for their policies to still remain active. Before any customer's policy lapses, the insurance company usually place calls across to the policyholder/life insured. They encourage policyholders to make payments before their policies lapse.

On the other hand, insurance companies believe that agents that have large number of their customers policies lapsed are not doing their jobs well. In managerial selection from ordinary agent, emphasis is laid on this. The company takes good look on the number of the customers' line of the agent whose policies have lapsed. If the agent has small proportion of his or her customers policies lapsed, he has higher chances of fitting into managerial position. But if it is the opposite, then there is problem.

An agent who has large number of his customers policies lapsed is poor in terms of customers' service. Such agent does not really have the capacity to manage customers well. To that effect, he will hardly manage group of salespersons properly.

Boldness and the ability to lead a Team

There are agents that are not bold in insurance companies. Any small issue with customers, the agents have already started panicking. Such agents are not bold and appear weak in the midst of their fellow salespersons. And as a result of this, this kind of agent may lack the ability to stand for his salespersons when appointed as a manager in any insurance company. He may end up giving the insurance company bad reputation.

Insurance management boards need agents that can represent their companies boldly. They need managers that are fearless. They appoint "lions" to lead a team of financial advisors in the industry and not cowards. They understand the importance of boldness which can take the company higher.

No matter how small the aspirant into managerial position may be, boldness can cover his small stature. They appoint people that can speak boldly to prospects and policyholders irrespective of who they are in the society. They do not want managers that will tremble when they hear that a particular dignitary is coming to visit the office.

The word "boldness" means willingness to take risks and act innovatively; confidence or courage. Before an agent is appointed a manager in insurance, these qualities are needed. The person is to be innovative and have the ability to take reasonable risk. These are the risk that can bring glory to the company. They are the risk that will make the company proud of having such manager.

Ability to lead a team is very important in insurance. When you are a good leader, you manage the people properly. But if you lack leadership quality, you cannot lead a group of persons. You are to manage people and not a person and because of that, the aspirant needs the ability to lead.

Leadership means the action of leading a group of people or an organization. Insurance companies do not want the behaviour of just one man's activity or actions. What the author mean is that risk management companies want someone who can work with the agents as a team to achieve results. They want managers that can reason with the agents to find out new ways to penetrate into the people and achieve good productivity performance. Insurance companies target more sales and believe they can achieve this result if managers can work as a team with the agents.

Managements in the insurance industry want ground breakers. They want people that when given the position of managers can break and wet the ground of the location they are with their teams. They want rugged managers and not those who are soft and lack ability to penetrate the areas they occupy.

That is one of the criteria insurance companies look at before selecting insurance marketers to lead a group as a unit manager. They want people that once in a while can take their agents out for marketing. They visit a particular location as a group and make the product the company sell known to large number of persons. They create awareness of the company's product to the people. This attitude can boost the sales of the products of the insurance company.

References

- Dan McCarthy (2018), How to Get Management Leadership Experience When You're not a Manager, published by Balance Careers, New York, United States

- Gulumser Murat, Roger S. Tonkin and D. Johannes Jüttner (2002), Competition in the general insurance industry, published by Springer, Berlin, Germany

- Gonzalo Vina (2017), Insurance Companies competing on Price and Value, published by Raconteur Media Ltd., Minories, London, England

- The Economic Times (2016), Definition of 'Lapsed Policy', Published by The Economics Times, New Delhi, India

Chapters 3

The Motivating Managers

The work is divided. Every manager has where he or she is gifted. As a leader has where he is good in, so are some insurance managers. The motivating managers are unique set of managers that insurance salespersons like working with.

These kinds of managers do not believe in impossibility. They do not believe in the "no business" ideology of many agents all over the world. That there are no businesses outside and that is why you are not productive is not for them.

They believe that no matter how rough the street is that you must have something to offer. There must be one or two persons to talk to and seal good deals. They believe so much in their philosophy about sales and that have been keeping them going.

Motivating managers can wake an unproductive financial advisors or salesman. These kinds of managers always have their ways of getting the job of this kind done. Even an insurance marketer who feels that he or she cannot do such job can be motivated and made to do the same job he has been complaining about in the time past. Many whom would have been lost in the insurance job have been brought back into the job again by this kind of managers.

If you are inspiring to find yourself as a salesperson in any insurance company, pray to find yourself under this kind of manager. They are loving people and they know the job. Such kinds of managers have ways to play on the emotions of the agents as well as that of the customers to make them active in the business of insurance again. There is no dull moment in working under such managers.

3.1 The Features of Motivating Managers

Insurance managers that are motivating have characteristics that they are known for. In this section, we will discuss the characteristics of this kind of leader.

Motivating Managers are focused

According Victor Lipman of Forbes, "If you're a manager and you're not motivating your people, you're not doing your job. At least not as well as it should be done" (Victor Lipman 2016). The journalist understands the benefit of motivation by managers and how it can help the managers get the expected result when they are focused.

Because motivating insurance managers are focused, they know what they want to achieve in the long run. Attitude of this kind make the employees under them to be focused as well. Also, it makes the agents to concentrate in their current job and give them no room to leave the company they work for.

This is in line with the statement of a professional manager, John L. Miller, he stated "Keeping your team focused and motivated is a key part of retention, and in ignoring these distractions" (John L. Miller 2017). He was talking about how employees leave their current place of work to another that pays better before he made the statement. From the manager's point of view, employees that have motivating managers hardly leave their current company to another one. Motivating managers are good leaders.

A true leader is expected to have some qualities. These qualities are what keep them going and enable them the ability to organize the people he or she leads. This is same with what is observed in motivating managers in the insurance industry.

A leader is the person who leads or commands a group, organization, or country. In insurance companies, a manager leads group of marketers or insurance agents. Both the manager and the agents are always facing heat from head office to meet their targets. Insurance job like any other marketing job is all about meeting target on weekly and monthly basis.

Some of the marketers at a point may like to leave the job because of the pressure that comes from the head office. Because motivating managers are empowering, they sometimes call the marketers that want to leave the job and motivate them. Through words of mouth and true encouragements, such agents get back to the job.

It appears to people as if such manager uses extra power, but they do not. It is what such managers have trained themselves in and they are good in that. They are just good in leadership position.

Motivating Insurance Managers retain Customers

Have you seen where a policyholder came into an insurance company's office to terminate his policy but ended up paying into the policy? It appeared as if it was charm but not so. Managers that can do that are usually good when it comes to motivation. They give you a thousand and one reasons why you have to allow the policy to keep running instead of terminating or stop making payments for the policies.

Improving customer retention can prevent billions of dollars of lost revenue in the insurance industry. Research from CallMiner revealed that avoidable churn costs businesses $136 billion in the U.S. alone. That is high.

Insurance companies frown at termination of an existing policy which has not attained maturity. Also, they do not want to see any of their policies lapse. As a result of that, customers' retention is priority. That is how motivating managers win the hearts of many customers by retaining them.

They motivate customers to keep on with the policies they have with their company. But unlike some managers that lack the ability to motivate some customers by words of mouth, they hardly retain customers. Some customers may come for termination but because such manager does not have the ability to convince and motivate the customer, they end up terminating the policy. And as termination is carried out, the company loses money. Not only that, it affects the score card of the manager.

3.2 How Motivating Insurance Managers keep Salespersons

It is not every insurance unit manager that has the ability to retain the marketers under them. Many managers lack the ability and end up losing agents that work under them. This makes them to continue recruiting new marketers' year in and year out. And one of the bad sides of this fresh recruitment of salespersons under certain managers is that the company's head office is not happy about that. Also, it affects the score cards of managers negatively.

Motivating managers are skilful when it comes to employees' management. They know how to guide and coordinate the young men and women under them. They are well gifted and properly understanding in some cases. They always have their ways on how to calm the staff under them down.

Many insurance agents who are doing well today in the insurance industry once wanted to leave their jobs. This usually happens at the beginning of the job when everywhere was rough. Agents in insurance companies really suffer at the beginning of their jobs.

The reason for this is because the job is commission based. At that point when they wanted to leave at the beginning, the reason is usually due to poor payment. They have not built their commission at that point and they face the temptation to leave the job and go for another job hunt where they have fixed salary.

At this time of trial, managers that are motivating never allow large number of their salespersons to leave their jobs as marketers. They always have their ways of motivating them to remain in the job. They paint pictures of the future glory in the job to the agents. They have many motivating tactics and can dish out any of them at any point in time just to keep the marketers in the job.

Salespersons in insurance companies are marketers. Sometimes these employees are broke financially and the motivating managers lend them some money. They do not motivate their new employees just with words of mouth but also with financial support. These managers are "correct leaders". They device ways to make the employees remain in their jobs irrespective of the problems and tough times they face.

Leaders in the highly competitive insurance industry should emphasize the importance to retain talented employees with managers in an effort to minimize costs and diminish productivity levels associated with employee turnover. The specific business problem was that some insurance managers lack strategies to retain talented employees (Marilyn Martin 2016). From the voice of Marilyn Martin, marketers who are talented in any insurance company have to be retained by the managers they work under. This will be an added advantage to the company in question. But it is unfortunate that not all managers have the strategies to retain employees under them. But motivating managers have the needed skills and strategies.

References

- John L. Miller (2017), The 6 Things I Do to Keep My Team Focused, published by Manuseto Ventures Inc., United States
- Marilyn Martin (2016), Strategies to Retain Employees in the Insurance Industry, publish by Walden University, United States
- Victor Lipman (2016), The Best Managers Motivate, published by Forbes Media LLC., United States
- Review Trackers (2019), How to Improve Customer Retention in the Insurance Industry, Published by Review Trackers

Chapter 4

The Bossy Managers

A bossy manager is that manager who is fond of giving people orders; domineering. This kind of manager sees his or herself as a mini god. The manager derives joy in giving command to the financial advisors under him or her. The agents under bossy manager have limits to what they say. They do not have such freedom of speech like when they are given the opportunity to work under a humble manager.

It is not as if these bossy managers are the best when it comes to productivity and results generation. The thing is that these are habits they developed over the years.

According to Lipman Victor, Founder and principal of Howling Wolf Management Training, LLC, "I've been reading with interest about Sheryl Sandberg's campaign to ban the word "bossy" - because of the negative implications it can have for young girls' feelings about future leadership. While I'm very sympathetic to Sandberg's message, there's another aspect of the word "bossy" that interests me even more. Too much management, or, more specifically, ineffective management - too often aka bossiness - is the enemy of productivity" (Victor Lipman 2015).

Lipman went further and said that the best managers create an environment where employees are confident to step out and take chances, not work in fear of mistakes. Here the great author and manager expressed his feelings on the negative effects of working under any bossy manager. It does not encourage productivity in any way. Bossiness has many negative effects on both the company and the employees.

4.1 Effects of Bossy Management on Insurance Agents

Working under a bossy manager is not something interesting in any way. The author has worked in office where he observed how some bossy managers treat the workers under them. Most agents that work under bossy managers are not finding anything interesting with such kind of management.

The agents do not work with their Full Minds

When a manager is bossy, she displays some attitudes that are not supposed to be so. She acts in irritating ways that disguises the insurance agents under her management. This makes the agents feel bitter in their minds. It makes them feel they do not suppose to be under such a manager.

In respect to this, they fail to work with their minds. They carry grudges and this has a way of affecting the way they carry out their duties as insurance agents negatively. They do not contribute their best in making sure that the units managed by such managers move forward.

To the agents, such manager needs to be demoted. "How can she be making us feel bad because she is our manager?" That is the voices of agents that work under such kind of manager. They complain always concerning the bad behaviour of their bad manager. They always check their wrist watches because they want to go home from the office. They want the work closing time to reach faster. They have no joy under her.

Salespersons Produce Lower

According to Ikhator Godwin of FBN Insurance, sales are emotional. If you are not happy with yourself, you will find it difficult to make sales. That was the voice of a motivating insurance manager speaking. A happy salesperson is likely to make more sales because he is happy. That is the mood of successful salespersons in any insurance company.

A bossy manager makes her salespersons angry. She has no motivation to give to the squad of marketers she manages to make them emotionally sound. As a result of this, the salespersons under her unit have low productions. When salespersons under motivating managers produce higher, those under bossy managers perform lower. The army of marketers under such manager are usually fed up with what comes out of her mouth.

A bossy manager can be insulting. She does not care to know whether the agents she insults are same age with her or older. To her, she can do anything because she is the boss of the unit. But little does she know that her bad attitude back fires. When she insults the agents, the agents will not produce effectively because the agents cry against her.

Every human deserves to be respected irrespective of the sex or age. This given respect makes us stay in peace and carry our tasks diligently. But little do bossy managers know about this. Some managers think it is by being harsh and shouting at their salespersons that will make them produce. That philosophy does not work. Excellence productions in insurance do not come that way.

At successful companies, employees have many to keep them busy. Having managers divert them into time-wasting activities cuts into productivity and works against the bottom line (Fraser sherman 2018). In this subject of discussion, the employees are the insurance salespersons working under various insurance companies.

Many bossy managers in the industry have diverted the attention of the marketers to something else. Some marketers under such managers are not productive again. Many of them are spending their time in search of another job due to the bad attitude of the bossy managers they work with. Some others waste their time doing irrelevant things because they are tired of working under bossy managers in insurance companies.

Job Frustration

Selling of insurance products is not like selling banking products or opening of bank accounts. In insurance, you pay premium to cover a particular risk or save money towards a particular plan. In ordinary account opening in banks, you can have access to your money in the bank any time you want. But this is not so in insurance. In insurance, you have to wait until the due time.

In some communities and countries, insurance contracts have bad reputations. Irrespective of the stress involved in selling insurance policies, some bossy managers add salt to the injury. From the commanding voices to threatening and the rest, they make the agents unhappy. They keep on threatening the agents under them that they will fire them. Even if the agent in question produced the previous week, they (the managers) do not want to know.

Attitude of this type makes some agents get frustrated on the job and apply for resignation to earn them small respect. The "bags of insults" that come from bossy managers has pushed many salespersons out of the job. Many have taken enough shit from such managers until they got to their breaking point. At that point they applied to quit.

According to Fraser sherman in her teaching on management, it is important to fix problems before the staff quits in frustration. But many bossy managers do not want to understand that. To some of them, they are gods and nobody should tell them what to do to increase productivity.

Imagine a bossy manager insulting you telling you that due to poor product that she imagines how you take care of your wife at home. Many bossy managers go as far as saying that. They can vomit any rubbish that comes out from their mouths without thinking twice.

The morale of many marketers is dead because of what they take from bossy managers. They wake in the morning and become frustrated because of the beast they will meet in the office. After moving on to a particular length, they get frustrated and quit the job that was putting food on their tables before.

4.2 Why Some Insurance Managers are Bossy

Something usually causes some kind things to happen. Also, some bossy managers in insurance offices act the way they do because of one or two reasons. Though such behaviour is not good because the best managers are not bossy, there are some factors that make them behave the way they do. Their controlling and rude attitudes to their agents have causes and origin. In this subheading, we will be discussing in detail why some managers are bossy.

Gender

Many female sales managers in insurance industry are the most with bossy attitude. They display this kind of rotten attitude not just to the agents that work under them but also to customers that visit insurance offices. Even some customers after visiting offices managed by female bossy managers are not happy to pick any other insurance policy with the company.

Many female insurance managers have the mentality that the best way to be respected by their agents is by being bossy to them. Being that they are women, they do not want anyone to disrespect them. So, they embrace a bossy attitude as one of the ways they feel they can earn respect to themselves.

This makes both the male and female salespersons under them to be afraid whenever they want to talk to such managers. They first of all weigh and organize what they want to say before they could talk to such female retail sales manager. The freedom to speak is not there because if you talk anyhow, you may end up getting rude answer from such manager. Not only that, you may get insulted.

Some female managers who are bossy do not joke. They do not smile when others are smiling because they are forming bossy person. They do not want themselves seen as other managers and yet they are not the best.

That is the philosophy of many female managers. "If I am not bossy, these my workers will not respect me enough" That is the reason behind what many of them do. But such is not bringing in good result and reviews to them. They are boring managers because they do not make anything about the job interesting. They are just like great oracles that sacrifices are offered to.

Wrong Orientation

What is orientation? Orientation is basic information or training that is given to people starting a new job, school, or course. It is a teaching that people believe and practice. It is what people have trained themselves on and find difficult to change as the life they live progress.

Wrong teaching in the world today has made a lot of insurance managers behave the way they do. Some managers are bossy because many people have educated them that the best way to get themselves respected in the insurance company is by being bossy. Many managers in insurance believe in this teaching and end up being bossy to both the employees and the customers.

Many have been living with this wrong orientation. They end up creating problems in the company instead of solving the challenges the company is facing. Wrong orientation is one of the reasons many insurance managers are not doing well. They practice the wrong orientation they were given instead of practicing what works in real life.

Pressure

Insurance job is about target. Nobody recognizes you when you are not doing well. Once you do below expectation as a unit manager, just know that the company will not be happy with you. Also, when this happen, you have to know that you may loss that unit you manage if you do not do what is expected of you from the company. You can be demoted and another person handed your unit to for better management.

As a result of pressure faced by managers in insurance companies, many have adopted the habit of being bossy. They have this attitude not because they just like being bossy but wanted to know if there will be improvement in sales by doing so. They think that being bossy will make the salespersons under them to make more sales. But in most cases that attitude does not give them the expected results.

Some of these managers call their marketers when they (the marketers) suppose to be resting at home asking of how many productions or proposal forms they have filled and paid for. Marketers or agents that do not give convincing number of closed businesses have it hot. They (the bossy managers) display their bossy attitude on phone. They may shout at the agents on phone telling them that if they do not get good number of closed businesses before the end of week that they will be issued query.

That is what pressure has turned many manager into. It is all about meeting target. It is either you meet the target or you are issued query. At the worst, such insurance agents get their sack letters.

Environment

Every environment has a way of influencing the people around it. The influence has a way of affecting the way we behave on our daily activities. A child that grows in cities is easily influenced by the city lifestyle and that which grows up in thick rural area has his behaviour influenced by the environment. The same applies to some managers in the insurance industry.

An interview to one manager on why she is usually harsh on the insurance agents under her said "I am hard to my agents because I grew up in a military environment. The environment influenced me and that is why many things about my leadership is command" That was the voice of one unit retail sales manager in FBN Insurance. According to her, her bossy attitude is because she grew up in military zone.

Sometimes, even before some managers that are bossy as a result of their old environmental can change. It will take time. It will take time for them to know the new and better ways of a good management. Sometimes people that act in bossy way do so without understanding that their attitudes hurt the people that work under them. It is not everyone that have strong mind when they were trained. In summary of this subsection, every bossy manager has something that makes him or she behaves the way he or she does. But that does not imply that being a bossy manager is good.

4.3 How to Work with Bossy Managers

Irrespective of the behaviour of many bossy managers, there are ways to work with them. In the other words, bossy managers' proper management is possible. This will prevent both the manager and the employees from having issues while working together. It prevents the employees from matching line when working with this category of persons.

When you handle these set of managers well, you will progress personally as an insurance agent. There are wisdom and skills to apply when working under this kind of manager. This will make you to still retain your job under them irrespective of the weak behaviour they display. Bossy managers may continue to display their bossiness but your ability to handle them can keep you going in the job.

Even though the words "boss" and "bossy" sound almost the same, they don't necessarily have the same meaning. In fact, a good leader is one who is adaptable, flexible, and ultimately empowers their employees. However, not all of us are that lucky. So, what do you do if you do not have one of those good kind of bosses? First things first: don't worry. There are things you can do to handle your bossy boss and still keep your sanity (Carol Morgan 2019).

Do not talk when they are talking

Just stay calm even if they are shouting at the top of their voice. Maybe something go wrong in the office and she is flamed up by such occurrence, just be mute and do not talk back. She is angry at that point in time trying to pour out her anger. Do not react at that point. Even if it seems she wants to block your eardrum with her shouts, do not talk back to her.

She will still calm down. That is what you see when you work with bossy female bosses. At that time she is angry she expresses her bossiness. You interrupting her at that point she shouts at the top of her voice makes her think that you are trying to reduce her power as the boss. So, do not try to add petrol to the already burning fire by responding to her verbally at that point.

Do as if you are a baby in her face when she talks out of anger. Even when she or he speaks to team of financial advisors in a meeting, do not interrupt. Allow the bossy manager to finish with all she or he wants to deliver. If the time for contribution comes, you can then say what you want to say.

Meet your Target

Managers are under the pressure of meeting their weekly and monthly target. That being said, bossy managers also share in the same pressure. Area sales managers call day in and day out to find out the performance of salespersons under them which bossy managers are among. Bossy managers become angrier when his or her unit is not meeting up with the average production given by the company.

If you want to be at peace with bossy manager, ensure you meet the target if you are under her. This will put smiles on her face and reduce her level of bossy attitude towards you. You two can even become friends when you always meet your weekly and monthly target. Even if you as a salesperson do not meet up with your weekly target every week, do not be the least performing salesperson in your unit. Always put in some efforts.

Know the Manager's Mood

It is very important to study a bossy insurance manager. This will go a long way to reduce some kinds of unnecessary furious reactions in her system. Gradually you study such manager to find what she likes and dislikes.

It is not every time you meet a bossy manager to complain or to help you solve issue customers complain. When a customer complains to you which maybe the payment she made into the company insurance account but is not reflecting in her policy statement and it requires you to take the complain to your manager, just know the best time to meet the manager for that. You do not have to meet your manager to solve such challenge when you know that the bossy manager is not in good mood. Apply wisdom while taking the challenge to her.

You can intelligently take the challenge to her when she is in good mood. You smile with her or wear good look as you present the issue to her. You can tell her that you want to take care of her lunch that afternoon. In the course of doing that, you pass the message across. She will gladly handle the issue for you.

References

- Victor Lipman (2015), The Best Bosses Aren't Bossy, published by Forbes, Washington Blvd, Jersey City, United States

- Fraser sherman (2018), What are the Effects of Bad Management on Employees, published by Hearst Newspapers, LLC, United States

- Ikhator Godwin, Motivation, Ekhator's Speech in FBN Insurance Unit Meeting, Delta State, Nigeria

- Carol Morgan (2019), What To Do If You Have A Bossy Boss, published by Life Hack, New York, United States

Chapter 5

Insurance Managers and Location

In choosing to work as a manager in any insurance company, location for the work matters a lot. Sometimes the location a manager chooses can go a long way in determining whether the manager will stand the test of time or not. Managers most times consider locations before they accept any managerial position from any insurance company.

There are many reasons managers consider locations before choosing to work as unit managers in many places. The reasons can be the peaceful state of the location, the business state, tribe, the nature of people occupying the place and the rest. All these reasons have one of two ways they affect insurance businesses. So, managers analyze all these before taking the offer to work as unit managers or not.

The Peaceful state of the Location

This is one of the things insurance managers consider before they choose to work in any location. No one will like to die carelessly for any organization because he or she wants to work. This being the case, insurance managers will not be happy to work in any environment that is not peaceful just because they need the money. That is a big risk.

Even though they work in the organization that deals on risk management, they will not like to die carelessly for the organization. They have their lives insured quite alright, but that does not mean they should just go out there and die carelessly because the insurance company they work for need some completed proposal forms submitted to make more money. First thing first and that first thing is the individual life protection of workers. Even if a manager dies in an environment that is not safe and the family of the manager paid huge claim too, the man will not be there to enjoy the money with the family. He is gone and no longer living.

In Nigeria for instance, many insurance managers working under insurance companies do not accept managerial positions to work in some places in northern part of the country. The reason is because of the crisis that has been going on in this part of the country. Some will say that they choose to be unemployed than to work in such location as managers.

Boko Haram has turned such location to a state of unrest. Boko Haram is a jihadist terrorist organization based in north-eastern Nigeria, also active in Chad, Niger and northern Cameroon. Killings have been going on in such location mainly in Yobe, Sokoto, Maiduguri and few parts of Kaduna of Nigeria. Due to this challenge, insurance managers will not like to find themselves in such locations. Man's life first before any other thing.

Business State of the Location

What does your insurance company sell the most? Do they specialize in selling life insurance products or mainly on general businesses? These are the things some managers put into consideration before choosing to find themselves in any location.

The business state of a particular community has a way of affecting a particular insurance company. The effect can be high in terms of selling insurance products and can also be low. The people that make up a particular area have a way of promoting a unit manager by high sales of insurance services or making the business of a particular insurance company hostile.

From my experience as an insurance salesperson, life insurance products sell more in an area occupied mostly by civil servants than in a location occupied by majority of businessmen and women. This scenario is based on Nigeria Experience. There are reasons behind these high sales of life insurance products in areas covered mainly by civil servants.

Civil servants easily consider signing up for products that allow them to save towards their retirement. These products are categorized under life insurance. They buy these services because they want to see what to fall back to at retirement. Unlike an average businessman, he will tell you that he prefers to put such money into business and make more money in return than to pay the money to insurance company in the form of premium.

All they think about is business and business most times. A typical businessman will tell you that he does not like the idea of tying down the money he wants to use for business. Some businessmen can even go as far as telling you that insurance companies are thieves. But civil servants at large do not react harshly to buying good savings plans from life insurance.

Education savings plans are another life insurance plans that many life insurance companies sell. Civil servants in large number buy this kind of product as well. They know as people that receive salaries every month, they need to be saving something aside for the future of their children. Primary and secondary schools education level may not be too stressful for them to take care of financially. Where the high financial demand comes in is during the higher education. In other to minimize this stress in terms of money demand, many civil servants buy education insurance policies from life insurance companies to save ahead of time.

In areas where buying and selling of business commodities by entrepreneurs is high, insurance managers whose company specialize in selling of general insurance services feel happy to be in those places. General insurance businesses are good for businessmen and women. Many business people buy such insurance products to have their businesses protected against the unforeseen circumstances. Prevention is better than cure and that is one of the reasons that make many entrepreneurs buy general insurance.

Some sign up for burglary insurance while others go for fire. Burglary insurance is good for many business owners. Burglary insurance is an insurance policy that provides financial compensation for loss or damage caused to property and valuable items due to burglary or house breaking (IIFL 2017). So, insurance manager location is affected by the nature of business that goes on in that location.

Also, insurance managers whose company special in selling of general businesses can do well due to sell of fire insurance services to entrepreneurs. Fire break out is something no one can predict. As a result of this, many entrepreneurs buy fire insurance for their businesses. Fire insurance is a property coverage that pays for damages to property and other losses you may suffer from a fire (Janet Hunt 2019). It can pay for the cost of repairing or replacing damaged property in your business or home.

From these analyses, the nature of jobs or businesses in a particular location has ways of affecting insurance managers. Managers that work in insurance companies that sell life insurance products are likely to do better in areas occupied by civil servants. On the other hand, managers that work in areas that have larger occupants of entrepreneurs whose insurance company specializes in selling of mainly general insurance products will excel in such location.

Tribe

What tribe is a particular insurance manager occupying? Also, which tribe is the manager that occupies such location? There is a saying that our own is our own. Such statement sometimes does wonders when it comes to insurance sales.

Sometimes it is easy for people to transact businesses with people they know than those they do not know. This applies to insurance management and businesses as well. If a manager speaks same language with the people in the community he manages, the manager is likely to make more sales in the company and prosper.

If he is from the same tribe with the location he occupies, he is likely to triumph as well. The reason is because he belongs to the people. Those who are not exposed in terms of formal education can easily communicate with the manager by their tribal language. So, it gives the manager the opportunity to grow in that location and have good stand as well. Language plays important role in business.

5.1 Location and Earnings in Managerial Offices in Insurance

In insurance, the location of any manager has some roles to play when it comes to earnings. In life in general, people who do business in rural areas do not rub shoulders with those that do their business in cities where there is more economic activities. Because of the high economic activities that go on in cities, the businessmen and women over there make more gains. They do more quality businesses because turnover is high. And those in rural towns do not make much gain due to low economic activities.

In insurance as well, location matters a lot. The location of a particular insurance manager has ways of determining how much he earns on monthly basis. He is likely to earn high when he works in offices located in cities with high economic activities. But if the manager is assign to stay in rural areas or places with less economic activities, he may earn lesser than those managers in the cities.

According to Glassdoor Company, in the US, there are insurance managers that earn salary of $80, 000/yr. But insurance managers that stay in rural areas can earn lesser than that amount. So the nature of the place insurance managers cover either affect their earnings in a positive or negative way.

So, if you are planning to assume a managerial position in your insurance career one day, also consider the location of the place you are going to. Also, ensure you consider the saturation of the area as well. What does the future of that place hold for you? Do you think that working in that location will help you grow your customers' base through your agents in the next 2 to 5 years? It is important to put that into consideration.

There are many people that have chosen a particular location to work as managers before now and they later found out the place has been saturated with other sellers of insurance policies. There are many other insurance companies in that location and making sales became difficult. The agents under the manager find it difficult to make sales because there are many other agents that sell similar products in that location. In return, this resulted to poor growth in the earning of the manager. Your location as an insurance manager also determines how much you take home.

Reference

- JANET HUNT (2019), What is Covered by Fire Insurance?, published by The Balance, New York, United States
- IIFL (2017), The Benefits of Burglary Insurance, published by India Infoline News Service, India

Chapter 6

Insurance Managers and Earnings

Many people have been making research over the years on how much an insurance manager in an insurance company is paid. There are statistics and data on those research works. The average salary for a Finance & Insurance Manager is $90,098 per year in the United States. The report was given by Indeed and last updated on October 22, 2019. As of Nov 5, 2019, Zip Recruiter reported that the average annual pay for an Insurance Manager in the United States is $73,294 a year. From those statistics, you will discover the differences. Some managers in insurance companies will not just disclose their salaries to people. In summary, all insurance managers do not have any fixed total earnings in a year.

But note that there are insurance companies that have fixed salary they pay to their unit managers which is different from the commission the managers will receive base on the earnings of the agents that work under them. An insurance manager in Nigeria for instance can receive a fixed salary of N150,000 (one hundred and fifty thousand naira) in a month. But his commission in that same month can be as high as N400,000 (four hundred thousand naira) in that same month. In most cases, commission received by insurance unit manager is higher than the basic salary or allowance as it is called as well.

Earnings serve as motivation to workers. Good earnings put smile on the faces of workers. It makes them happy because it is an evident that they are productive in their work. But poor earning do not motivate employees and make them sad. It makes them feel as if they have been wasting their time in their places of work.

Earnings simply mean money obtained in return for labour or services. Insurance managers are paid by insurance companies they work for. It is through the money they receive that they use to take care of themselves and their families. A retail sales manager in insurance company will like to earn well and grow in the company he works in for higher promotion as time goes on. That is why insurance managers put in all they have to make sure they meet their target and drive the market.

6.1 How much does an Insurance Manager Earn?

This question has been answered briefly before now but we are going to discuss more on it. This is a common question that people ask both online and offline. The author of this book has been asked this question by people on many occasions. Sometimes he answers and sometimes he may not depending on the reason why the person asks such question. Anyway, you never can tell whether the persons that asked such questions are planning to become managers in any insurance company one day.

Anyway, the simple answer to that question is that there is no specific amount of money an insurance manager earns every month or every year. Insurance managers do not have any fixed amount they can earn on monthly basis. They may have a basic salary that each unit manager earns in a particular company so far he meets his monthly target but that is not all each insurance unit manager earns in a month. **Manager A** can earn $6,600 in a month and **Manager B** can earn the same $6,600 in that same month as basic salary.

But the variation comes due to commission paid. Insurance managers earn by commission and that is the reason why it is like that. There are top performers in insurance managerial positions and there are those that perform on average level. Also, there are those that perform below average as well. How much an insurance manager earns is dependent on some basic factors.

6.2 Channels Insurance Managers earn

Every manager in insurance industry has avenues they are paid on monthly basis by the company they work for. After the summation of the total earnings channels, that forms their earnings for the month. The money they earn can come bit by bit but at the end you find out that is good sum of money the managers earn in a month.

In this section, we will be discussing how unit sales managers in insurance earn their money every month. According to Careerizma, insurance managers earn their remuneration from three sources: a salary, overrides on the sales made by their agents at their branch office, and commissions on sales made by the manager themselves (Careerizma 2015). We will restructure these avenues into three basic channels:

- From allowance/Salary
- From Agents sales and
- The Managers existing businesses

From Allowance/Salary

There is basic allowance that every manager is entitled to earn every month so far the manager meets up with the number of monthly cases and premium stated by the company. This standard is different per company. In a life insurance company in Nigeria, for any Tier 2 unit manager to be paid a complete allowance of one hundred and fifty-five thousand naira in a month (N155,000), the unit manager must produce at least 160 proposal forms through the agents that work under him every month. Also, the total premium paid on the new sold policies for that month is not to be less than about four million five hundred thousand naira only (N4,500,000). This makes him entitled to that amount of money. If he does not meet up with that target, then the allowance will still be paid to him but will not be complete.

Other insurance companies also have the standard they set for their individual managers to be entitled to complete basic allowance or salary. So, all insurance managers working in an insurance company will not have the same amount of salary/allowance every month. Those that did not meet up with the standard set by the company will be paid their salaries according to how they produced. The job is all about target.

From Agents Sales

How many cases each agent that makes up a manager's unit produce is another determinant to how much a manager takes home every month. A manager that has active and productive salespersons can earn more than other managers. For each premium paid by a policyholder, agent is paid commission on that. As the agent earns commission from those premiums, the manager earns as well.

An agent may be paid 10% of the premium paid by the customer and the manager of that agent paid 5% of the premium. But the percentage rate is based on the type of product. If a customer for instance pays premium of $500 and the rate for the agent commission is 10%, which means that the agent is entitled to $50 from the premium paid by that customer. In the same line, the manager of that agent gets $25.

Let us say that the agent has 200 customers that pay the same amount at the same commission rate, which will be a good amount of money for him as well as his manager. As he grows in earnings, his manager grows. If the manager has 20 salespersons under him and the whole twenty are as active as the person used in the example, which means he will earn something good from the sales of the agents at the end of the month.

The Managers Existing Businesses

Many managers were once ordinary salesmen. So before they were promoted to the positions of managers, they have many customers base they were managing. They were the people those customers call for anything concerning their policies. So when they got promoted to the position of a manager, they still have some customers that they opened policies for who still pay their premiums as of when due.

Those policies are known as initial existing businesses. So, that the former salespersons are now managers do not stop them from earning commission from those businesses. When those old customers pay premiums, the managers are paid commission on them. An insurance manager has many outlets he earns from every month.

The earnings when summed together answers the question of how much an insurance manager earns every month. So, there is no specific amount of money an insurance manager earns every month. The earnings vary because of the way they are paid. But the fact remain that they are big officers in insurance companies and many of them earn well. Managers often view salary as part of a total compensation package that includes benefits, bonuses, incentive pay, perks and other reward tools (Brain Bass 2011).

6.3 Factors Affecting Earnings of Insurance Managers

In the field of insurance and earnings, there are some factors that play important roles on whether managers earns high, moderate or low. These factors have been playing their roles in insurance managerial positions for years. These are the factors that differentiate one insurance manager from the other.

The factors affecting the earnings of insurance managers are as follow:

- Experience in the job and skills
- Agents performance
- Location
- The insurance company's brand

Experience in the job and Skills

A manager that is experienced in the managerial position can win more insurance businesses for his salespersons thereby increasing his own earnings. Experience as being said is the best teacher. That same statement works well in determining how much an insurance manager earns every month as a reward for the good job he has been doing for the insurance company.

Many managers that are doing better than some others sometimes find themselves in that state because of their sound level of experience in the job. There are managers that have stayed up to 6 years in their managerial position in an insurance company. Also, there are those that have stayed for just one year. Between these two groups of managers, they cannot earn the same amount of allowance every month. That who has stayed more years in the company will have higher basic allowance than the one that has handled the position for just a year. The manager that has stayed in the company for a year can be a tier 1 manager while the one that has worked for six years can be a tier 3 manager. The difference is clear and so their individual basic salaries and commission.

Also, there are insurance managers that are more skilful than the others. They use their skills to get more businesses and increase their earnings. They also can teach the agents under them on how to use these skills to make people sign up for more insurance policies. Motivating and empowering managers sometimes earn more than those that lack such skills.

Agents Performance

In football especially in football clubs, most times when a team is not doing well, the blame is usually shifted to the football club coach. The reason is because the coach is the person that trains the footballers and tells them what to do on the pitch. But if a coach does well and has his team doing well, the credit does not just go to the footballers but also the coach. It is a way of saying that the coach is doing well and that can lead to promotion. And when a coach is promoted, he earns higher than before as wage.

In the field of insurance managerial positions, similar thing still occur. When the agents that work under a manager are performing well, the manager can be promoted. Not that the manager will just be promoted but he will earn more money as salary every month. There are agents that really do better than others in terms of closing more businesses and in customers' service relationship.

They motivate prospects so easily to open more policies. Tell them the reasons why they have to do so and before you know the business is sealed. Such agents are exceptional and they put smiles on the face of their manager. The manager smiles because he knows he has agents that are doing well and can make him earn better as salary and commission.

When a manager has 10 of that kind of salespersons, he will earn well. But if the salespersons under a manager are not performing well, the manager will not earn well. As a result of this, his earning will not be high.

Location

As explained in the previous chapter, location contributes to how much money an insurance manager will go home with at the end of every month. The location of an insurance branch is a particular place is an important determinant on whether the manager is to be classified among the top earners in the industry or not. How much awareness do people staying in that location have on insurance? Do they see insurance as something nice to go into or as scam? There are some places where people see insurance as scam because the insurance companies located in those places do not usually pay claim.

The earnings of insurance managers in United States of America cannot be the same with that of managers in Nigeria. A lot of factors can be the reasons for that. Insurance penetration in the United States of America is far higher than that of Nigeria. Large population of Americans are aware of insurance and they see it as contracts that are worth entering into. Some of the citizens even market for insurance companies that have paid them claim before free of charge because they are happy.

In Nigeria, some people look at you as a foreigner when you mention insurance in their face. They see you as someone that does not know what he is saying. They may start by asking you to explain what you mean by insurance. Their knowledge on insurance is limited and sales in this kind of location are low. What it implies is that the insurance managers in this location will earn lower than those in the United States.

Another thing to consider when it comes to location is the stability of the economy in that location. Is there high inflation rate in that location or not? Some intelligent people in some locations consider some factors before investing their money in insurance. They think about many things including inflation.

Managers in communities where there is inflation earn lesser that those managers that stay in countries with no or low inflation. Inflation reduces the value of money. A society that has high inflation rate will have low investors in long time policies. People that suppose to buy insurance for retirement like personal retirement plans or annuity may not because they know that if they save for long using insurance, the money will lose value at maturity. What $6 can buy today $8 may not be able to buy in the next ten years.

These issues arise due to high inflation rate in some countries. People prefer to use their money today than to buy annuity insurance policy today and hence do not enjoy the proceeds of the policy tomorrow because the money loses its value. United States, Canada, Italy and other countries are doing well in insurance today because of their stable economy. But in Africa and few other countries, insurance do not sell well. As a result of this, location determines how much an insurance manager earns on monthly basis.

The Insurance Company's Brand

There are many insurance companies but some have better positive ratings than others. Insurance companies that are rated high have ways it affects the income of the managers that work under them. Those insurance companies are regarded as the giants among other insurance companies in that location. They usually receive good reviews from people.

When people hear about the companies' name, they feel pleased to buy insurance products from them. As they buy more policies, the managers expand their incomes. So, the companies have better brand names. They easily attract more policyholders to their companies.

There are some insurance companies that emerge from existing parent companies. Example is the one in Nigeria called FBN Insurance. The name FBN stands for First Bank of Nigeria. FBN has good reputation and has lasted in the country for over 125 years. The company has positive reviews from customers.

Being a financial institution that has been into finance business for years, people feel happy to do business with them. When First Bank of Nigeria created its new insurance arm called FBN Insurance, many Nigerians felt happy to buy products from the insurance company. They believe that since the parent company which is the bank has been doing well, the insurance company will not fail.

Within less than 10 years of the existence of FBN Insurance, they have stood their ground. The company has good customers base which they build within few years because of the brand name "FBN" The management of the company has experience in risk management. Managers of FBN Insurance earn much higher than those in other insurance companies in Nigeria. This is so because the company has good brand name and has built their customers base and are still growing in insurance business.

References

- Careerizma (2015), Insurance Manager, published by Careerizma, India
- Brain Bass (2011), The Advantages of the Managerial Compensation of a Fixed Salary, published by Chrone, New York, United States
- Indeed (2019), Finance & Insurance Manager Salaries in the United States, published by Indeed website, United States
- Zip Recruiter (2019), Insurance Manager Salary, published by Zip Recruiter Inc, California, United States

Chapter 7

Insurance Managers and Market Drive

Among the functions of an insurance manager is to supervise and drive market. He directs and observes the execution of a task. And the task here is to make sure that the insurance company makes more sales that can lead to their growth. In each country, there is competition among insurance companies. Every of the insurance companies want to be referred to as number one.

Even in a particular insurance company, the managers compete among one another. They want to be regarded as number one. Any that does not do well this week through his productions report for the week works hard to make sure that he performs better next week.

That is the drive among insurance managers. Any manager that allows his drive for the insurance business dies off will not be happy with his or herself in the long run. That is because when others whose drive is still active are rewarded by the company for doing exceptionally well, such manager will not be recognized. It is usually shameful and challenging.

In some insurance companies, managers receive awards every month for being the number one in any month. That is motivation and any of the managers that are awarded for high productivity will not like to fall back. He will rather like to retain the position for second or third time. It is motivating and human in general feel happy to be honoured for something he or she does well.

Insurance managers who are passionate about their jobs integrate the good spirits into their agents. They make the agents that work under them to see the beauty of the job they do and produce more. They have the skills they teach the agents that work under them for them to do well.

7.1 How Insurance Managers Drive Market

There are number of ways insurance managers drive market. The ways are as follow:

- Motivating the agents
- Strategic marketing
- Support during marketing
- Supervising the agents

Motivating the Agents

One of the ways insurance managers win more businesses for the insurance companies they work is by motivating their agents. They make them understand that there is nothing they cannot achieve in the insurance agency job. This sometimes moves the agents to do more in the business to make more money for themselves.

Every insurance agent feels happy when their managers make statement like this "you can go home with at least five figure earnings on monthly basis as commission". Statement like this usually triggers agents in insurance industry to go out there and make more sales. They use all the necessary skills they have to convince most people they come across to buy insurance policies they sell for their companies.

The drive first starts when the managers of their units motivated them. It is this motivation that adds extra energy to them for more outstanding result. Motivation is powerful and this is what many managers in the insurance company had used to achieve something great. Many managers that outshine others are good motivational leaders.

Motivation is the word derived from the word 'motive' which means needs, desires, wants or drives within the individuals. It is the process of stimulating people to actions to accomplish their goals. This is what many insurance managers do. When they motivate their agents, they empower them and hence win more business for the insurance company.

The goal during motivation is to make sure that many policyholders are brought into the insurance company. When many agents are motivated by their managers, the managers make them understand that when they sell insurance policies to customers, they sell value to them. Let the people see what you are selling to them as value and not just mere insurance policies. This is usually part of their statements.

They take this message out there to them. When they the prospects understand that what they are persuaded to buy are values and not just mere insurance policies, they sign up. As the insurance company make more sales, they make more profit. At the end, the managers that drive the market more than others through their agents via motivation or motivating their agents are recognized by the company.

The recognition can come in the form of award at the end of each business year. When they recognize these outstanding managers, they are motivated as well to do more in the coming years. Also, the outstanding insurance agents that help the managers in market drive are also recognized. Recognition of insurance companies' managers through award giving has brought competition in the industry. This is a good way to promote the insurance industry.

Strategic Marketing

This is another way insurance managers' drive market in the insurance industry. Strategic marketing is a process of planning, developing and implementing manoeuvres to obtain a competitive edge in your chosen niche. They plan on areas to go and make sales with their agents. They do not just move instead they sat down and make the plan for effective result.

They take some agents to a particular location to cover that area and take others to another location to cover as well. They teach their agents different technique to apply in the individual locations that will work. The tactics that work in location A may not work in location B. So they know what to apply to get the expected result in any particular area of coverage.

During strategic market driven by insurance managers, meeting customer needs a likely and attainable goal. The managers make this happen through their agents. When they take their salespersons to a particular location, they tell them the kind of insurance products to sell to the people in that particular area. These are the products that must meet the needs of the people occupying that area.

When the prospects see that the policies they are motivated to sign up for will go a long way to help them achieve their life goals, they have no option than to sign up for them. These are policies that were design with the mindset to tackle particular needs of the people. So, insurance policies are nice and suit the individual needs of the people.

If the manager for example decides to take his team of salespersons to universities for instance to target the workers in that place, the main product he may plan to be sold to the people can be retirement and annuity policies. This will meet the needs of the workers in the long run. If the target is the students, insurance savings plans with little risk premiums become the best. At the end, the manager will drive the market with the sell of many policies.

Support during Marketing

There were occasions when prospects were brought in an insurance office and the manager did like he did not know that a prospect was there. The prospects were brought in by the agent under his unit. He the manager sometimes did not like to contribute to the way the agent in his unit marketed to the prospects. In most cases, this is common with bossy managers.

On the other hand, there is insurance manager that feels happy when his agent brings in prospects into the insurance office. The manager being more experienced in the job than his agent joins his voice to market to the prospects in a more convincing way. In fact, at the end, the prospects sometimes pick more insurance policies than the one he would have picked because the whole job was not left for the agent to do all alone but the manager contributed.

Managers' support to the salespersons have proven to be one of the ways to win more businesses for insurance companies. It is one of the ways some managers drive insurance market in their respective locations. A manager that wants to drive market does not always stand and observed when their agents are marketing customers. They come in when there is difficulty to win the business for the company. Sometimes, salespersons go to some organizations for presentation. They first wrote to the targeted organization and they are called later by the organization in question to present their products which are insurance policies. Understanding managers in some cases go with the agents to the place of the presentation on that day. It is not as if the agents could not do the job if they are left alone to go for the presentation.

The manager's presence can spice things up. And because the main goal for the product presentation is to make sales, the manager follows to make sure that the aim is achieved. He makes sure that the mission is accomplished by driving the market. He wants to make more sales and be recognized by the company for outstanding performance.

Supervising the Agents

Because of the way insurance agency job is, sometimes some fulltime agents are not serious with their jobs. They pretend as if they are working while they are not doing anything. They lose focus and may divert their attentions to something else. They become poor performers when it comes to marketing and submitting proposal forms to the insurance offices for capturing and conversion.

In a highly competitive market such as the insurance business, measuring sales performance precisely and rapidly can determine the knife-edge difference between profitability and loss-making decisions. Belgian insurance company DVV, part of the Dexia Group, clearly understands this. They realized that they needed fast and accurate sales and customer portfolio information (SAS Institute Inc 2006).

When managers supervise their agents when they are in the field, it helps them to find out those who are working and others that are not. Through this means, they discover the new approach they will apply to tackle the issue. Sometimes they hold meeting with these agents to find out what is really the issue. Some of them may be emotionally down and the lasting solution to such agents issue is usually to discuss with them and know the way forward.

Also, many agents usually lose interest on the job after weeks of dry sales. The best thing managers usually do to make them to still like the job is to motivate them. Sometimes they go out with such agents to market in the field. Managers that do not monitor their agents may not discover these flaws on time.

The essence of the supervising is to know how to help these agents and still ensure market drive. When these agents start working well again, they become exceptional in their jobs. Also, they begin to like the job they do as well. When everyone in the unit is performing well, there will be achievement of outstanding results. This is how many managers in the insurance industry have driven insurance market over the years.

According to Gnosis, insurance industry shall manage more effectively their operations, manage risks and grow through Strategic Performance Management. Performance is important and it is used to rate insurance companies in different countries. Any insurance company whose agents perform low on average is not rated high. To avoid low rating by the regulatory body, the need to direct agents per company by their managers come into play. Monitoring of agents has proven to be one of the lasting solutions to drive insurance sales.

Any insurance company that wants to survive in the insurance industry must not allow their powerhouse to be weak. The powerhouse of every insurance company is the agents. When the agents are weak, the company becomes weak. To avoid this from happening, they should be checked on always.

References

- Gnosis (2014), Insurance Performance Management System, published by GNOSIS Management LTD, Strovolos, Cyprus
- SAS Institute Inc (2006), Close monitoring of Insurance Agents helps ensure Success, published by SAS Institute Inc, Carolina, United States

Other Books by the Author

- Choosing and Working as an Insurance Agent by Uzochukwu Mike P
- Insurance Prospects and Customers: Understanding Insurance Policies by Uzochukwu Mike P

www.ingramcontent.com/pod-product-compliance
Lightning Source LLC
Chambersburg PA
CBHW020607220526
45463CB00006B/2495